OBJECTS HEAVY IN THIS LIFE

poems by

Clare Chu

Finishing Line Press
Georgetown, Kentucky

OBJECTS
HEAVY
IN
THIS
LIFE

Copyright © 2022 by Clare Chu
ISBN 978-1-64662-859-9 First Edition
All rights reserved under International and Pan-American Copyright Conventions. No part of this book may be reproduced in any manner whatsoever without written permission from the publisher, except in the case of brief quotations embodied in critical articles and reviews.

ACKNOWLEDGMENTS

These poems first appeared in print or online in the following journals:

Breathe: "Confinement"
Cagibi: "Palimpsest," "Sticks and Stones"
The 2River View: "27359"
The Esthetic Apostle: "Driving on Pico Blvd." "Losing Friends at Age Six"
The New Guard: "We Will Not Be Quiet"
The Raw Art Review: "The Pickling of Limes"

Publisher: Leah Huete de Maines
Editor: Christen Kincaid
Cover: *Four Phases of the Moon*, Justen Ahren, www.justenahren.com
Author Photo: Clare Chu
Cover Design: Elizabeth Maines McCleavy

Order online: www.finishinglinepress.com
also available on amazon.com

Author inquiries and mail orders:
Finishing Line Press
PO Box 1626
Georgetown, Kentucky 40324
USA

Table of Contents

Death by Drowning 1
March 16, 2020 2
Escape 3
27359 4
Incubus 5
Sticks and Stones 6
The Last Tip 8
Lies Women Believe 9
My Shelf 10
Losing Friends at Age Six 11
Live Wire 12
Objects Heavy in This Life 13
Palimpsest 15
The Pickling of Limes 16
Fourteen Ways of Looking, By a Rhino 17
Fornicating Pigeons 19
Let Not Light 20
Divorced Because of Poetry 21
Have You Ever? 23
Perpetually Unmasked 25
Case # 1803 27
Driving on Pico Blvd. 29
We Will Not Be Quiet 30
Confinement 31
Emergency Room 32
The Reckoning 33
New California 34

*Sometimes you are erased before you are given
the choice of stating who you are.*
    —Ocean Vuong, On Earth We're Briefly Gorgeous

DEATH BY DROWNING

If you commit suicide in your pool, it will be drained and used as a temporary gravesite, said the letter from the Department of Unforeseen Deaths. *Not just for you, we will commandeer it for those people who do not have the luxury of drowning in their own pools. Furthermore, we can't promise that family members that die together will be buried together.*

That evening, the police flew an army of drones over Southern California to monitor the rapidly developing situation. Dimly lit by stars, hundreds of bodies floated face down. Hundreds of pools, arms outstretched. There was no need to touch.

No notes left for loved ones. The interminable shock, deeper than any pool.

Media reports, in real-time, stated that deranged introverts, left to their own devices for too long, stripped naked, and jumped into their pools. Extroverts danced to the point of death before they gyrated into the water. Some howled and shouted obscenities at the sky.

It was announced that the immediate families of those heard cursing would lose their death benefits. Neighbors were urged to spy on 'drowners', to call 1-800-CORPSES for a reward.

The next day, throughout the state of Florida, more bodies from more pools were recovered. And the day after, even more, discovered in Maryland, then Oregon and Texas. Save for the Strasbourg dancing plague of 1518, psychologists had little research to call on, a lack of precedent to follow.

The government makes it clear that this type of collective behavior will not be tolerated. Think very carefully about the consequences of your actions. Don't be selfish. No one should have to speculate about the loss of their loved one. Failure to drown is a felony, punishable by house arrest.

Death by drowning is now against the law in all fifty states.

MARCH 16, 2020

It's not as though it's Ebola,
Beverly says. She cradles
a crumpled plastic bag in her arms.

They're eggplants,
I hope you're not allergic.

Despite my request,
she refuses to put the bag by the door.

I can't bend down, dear,
not with my back these days.

Beverly shoves the bag towards me,
forces me to take it,
freed, she exhales loudly.

She stands two feet from me,
I back up, praying she won't take this
as an invitation to enter my house.

I thank her for her gift.
I look at the bag I'm holding.

I look at the sweat on her upper lip.
I try not to breathe.

Beverly turns, leans on her stick,
walks slowly down my drive.
I wonder if I thanked her enough.

And, as I lock my door,
I wonder if,

fresh from New York,
I've just signed her death warrant.

ESCAPE

After I couldn't bear to listen to my husband droning on and on all day about the weather, about his old job, about how overworked he'd been for years, I suggested we learn German online. I knew how difficult the grammar was, how hard it would be for him to produce the guttural sounds—he had no ear for language and was losing his hearing to boot. Sunday was designated 'German' day. It soon became the most peaceful day of the week.

Of course, it made his tedious complaints stand out the other six days, so I decided we should learn Welsh next. We spoke only Welsh on Wednesdays. Then I added Turkish on Thursdays and soon Spanish on Saturdays. At last, the house was quiet.

We got used to the silence. As 'Shelter-in-Place' went from weeks to months to years, we forgot how to speak English, so took a Zoom course in 'Casual Conversation' but even everyday English on Fridays was monosyllabic now.

One Monday I looked across the room at his perfectly knotted tie, saw confusion in his clenched teeth, reticence in his locked jaw. He could no longer remember what day of the week it was, and in which language he could communicate with me.

27359

> *Until 1913 when the practice was abolished,*
> *prisoners in Lisbon Prison had to wear a hood*
> *whenever they were in a communal space.*

I lost my name, became a number,
was given a hood to wear.

Obliterated by the absence of light
I confront you from within.

> You do not know where to look—
> yet you cannot look away.
>
> You are crushed by my face
> concealed in the darkness.
>
> All you can imagine is your own face.

There is a sameness in my world
in the space where shadow meets light,
light meets shadow.

There is a pause in penetrating a minute.
I do not know where to look—
reality laps at the edges of my life.

I feel suffocated. I am in a hood,
beside a hood, overlooking a hood.

I am a hood.

INCUBUS

I hear you from my bedroom, closing our house down for the night, though I have already drawn the curtains, turned off the lights in the room where we no longer sit together. You still cling to me though, a wounded predator that has sunk his teeth into his prey.

Since I moved myself into the guest room, you don't remember to lock the back door before you come up, though we both know when I find it open in the morning, I will be mortally afraid.

Of course, the night terrors have returned—they lie in wait, clustered between bookshelves in the corner of the room, for that moment when I fall into sleep. What am I now willing to receive in the bed that was never ours?

The Mockingbird outside my window sings at nighttime in endless rising tones. Like it, I want to flaunt my agony through another's song. I want to tell you not to press your hand upon my chest, because in my paralysis, I won't be able to feel you.

Your tread on the stairs is no longer quiet, your step just so deliberate. Before you go into our room and settle into our bed, you pause and cough once, some nights twice, outside my door.

STICKS AND STONES

Kerfuffle—
    as in:
        She causes a kerfuffle dancing on the bar,
        as he follows her, he tells himself she's asking for it.

Riven—
    as in:
        She lies under a tree riven by lightning, says nothing—
        his hand over her mouth, the other at her throat.

Arrest—
    as in:
        Her fragrance is arresting when he pushes his head
        between her breasts and bites her.

Iota—
    as in:
        She doesn't give one iota afterward her dress is bloody,
        she will never wear it again.

Maudlin—
    as in:
        Her mother spoke sharply: *you've been maudlin ever*
        since—you need to snap out of it.

Gossamer—
    as in:
        She reads in a book her hymen was as thin as gossamer
        and shaped like a crescent moon.

Echo—
    as in:
        The jury's silence echoes around the courtroom when
        she stumbles through the events of that evening.

Stagger—
> as in:
>> The judge is staggered her mother allows her out on a school night, suggests the girl is out of control.

Abject—
> as in:
>> Abject after his acquittal, she ditches school to buy a rope, looks up online how to tie a noose.

Predispose—
> as in:
>> The papers report there is nothing in the family history of the victim that predisposed her to hang herself.

THE LAST TIP

Grace leaves the club, the echoes of a saxophone
float under her hat,
the streetlight's glare cut off by its brim.

In the drawn-down-dark of nightfall,
Frank sleeps at an angle by a flophouse door,

body and arms wrapped square
'round a pillow she tossed his way last week.

Grace fishes in her coat for a small bill—
eggs and a biscuit for his breakfast.

Frank takes the bill, mutters his thanks,
slips the pillow behind his back.

Too late, she realizes her last tip
was a fifty, tucked under her garter
by one of her regulars.

Back home Grace downs whiskey with a Miltown chaser,
stows her cash in a babushka nesting doll
that reminds her of her grandmother, her mother, her aunt,

her sister who threw herself out
of their fourth story window
a week before Grace ran away the first time.

That night she dreams Frank is smothered
by his pillow, left for dead,
for fifty dollars he never knew he had.

LIES WOMEN BELIEVE

Your body is a temple,
he whispers,
to be worshiped and adored.

Eagerly I purify it
for him, jettison the
flotsam, the jetsam.

Reject debris, odds
and ends, bibs and bobs,
rising to the surface.

I look at my atoned self
at the bare bones—
without envy.

I need my rage.
I want to reclaim the fire
of my unzipped life.

In my longing,
piece by piece,
I salvage myself.

MY SHELF

My shelf is a city, sadness for miles,
chipped cups, a journal, chocolate to share,
urban decay, dreams lying in dust piles.

Erect, on the left, stale perfume vials
beside Lord Wellington, mad lonely bear,
my shelf is a city, sadness for miles.

Ceramic-veiled nuns prostrate in the aisles,
silver-framed Marilyn, skirt in the air,
urban decay, dreams lying in dust piles.

Invitations in alphabetical files,
The Joy of Sex next to a book of prayer,
my shelf is a city, sadness for miles.

Three pairs of shoes in yesterday's styles,
a tarnished locket of wispy blonde hair,
urban decay, dreams lying in dust piles.

Is life to be a series of trials?
Each day, for the most part, I go nowhere,
my shelf is a city, sadness for miles,
urban decay, dreams die in dust piles.

LOSING FRIENDS AT AGE SIX

Jane was the first to go. I imagined she slipped through a rent in the sky one morning when the air was too thin, but afterward, we walked to school in pairs. Our mothers said, *Never to talk to strangers*. I became mouse-silent—my strangers at home, in furled disguise, until evening dusk erased their stark smiles.

Oliver was next. My mother said, *Pour me another for the road*, and one street over his mother said, *Curiosity killed the cat*, so Oliver went in search of his missing, likely dead, cat. Climbed over the backyard fence, snagged his sweater on the wire, licked the blood from his wrist, and made a break for it down the grass bank. Disappeared under our weaving car. Mother never saw him coming.

Finally, small Silvia, our 'baby' in the game of 'mothers and fathers,' not allowed to play with us after she ran from her mother one day, through a glass door that splintered, turning her hair white overnight. And forever mouthed strange things to me from across the street, like *We will meet as birds with open wings*, before she too vanished, through the same seamless tear in the sky.

LIVE WIRE

From   day   one
                            yelling
like nobody's business
a vision of fury—

born a live wire

I retreat   silent
I grow up   frozen

Do what you want
because you always do
      you always will

trying hard   be good
trying hard   get God

arms outstretched
face down—
I lie on the floor

beg Father
to admit
I am adopted

If her perm wasn't soldered
to her head
Mother would've pulled her hair out

Do what you want to me—
all of you—because
      you always do
      you always will.

OBJECTS HEAVY IN THIS LIFE

We Leave Ourselves in Each Room of the House.

On the back of every tongue in my family is the will to be unheard. In between bites, we are expected to converse, yet say nothing. Nothing in our house is allowed to be dirty, especially not our words. No 'lavatory' humor. One evening, my throat closes. Not permitted to speak with my mouth full, I chew, until meat turns to gristle, turns to leather. It takes many years to learn how to swallow.

*

No Longer in the Loop.

Sundays we walk in line to church, Mother at the front, my sister at the rear. One week Mother feels 'off-color.' For Father, that's an excuse to stay home, to phone his secretary from his study. I interrupt him, tell him it's time to go. He yells, *Get out and exercise those muscles.* I do. I run the whole way to avoid the tramp who lives on the other side of the dry-stone wall. Mother tells me he is known as "Woodcrutch Joe." He has one good leg. I should've prayed for him.

*

The Long Blade of Light.

Father gives me a wind-up clown with a painted porcelain face. The crooked index finger on its left hand points at me from the high bookshelf in my bedroom, where it is placed to surprise me. At night under the moonlight, the clown's face glows. I wonder what I've done to deserve such a gift from Father.

*

Don't Let Grief Catch Up. Run Faster.

The joy of belonging to a family is lost overnight. Father's long-time affair with his secretary is discovered. I come home from school to find Mother sitting on the carpet, legs splayed, beside a bottle of scotch, a pair of scissors in her hand. I watch in silence as she cuts up the bedsheets.

*

Ashes of Roses.

She may well be a saint, the women at the Methodist Church say of Mother, who brings food to "Woodcrutch Joe," buys flowers for the church, volunteers at the library on Saturday mornings when children fill the story-telling room. *Why do you do it all?* I ask her, *Does it make you happy? Quite the opposite,* she replies, then leaves on another goodwill errand.

*

I Reach For You As I Shed My Skin.

My little sister is always late. One day, instead of taking her to school, I leave her sleeping and take my ventriloquist dummy, Doris. Her teacher is not amused when I march in and sit Doris down on the front row. *You Jenkins girls are monsters,* she shouts. I head off to my own classroom.

*

I Unpack Myself. Unpack My Lies.

My sister's lack of punctuality continues into adulthood. She makes it to the tail-end of Father's wedding reception when he marries his secretary, but not to the church. We go to her place afterward, get drunk on Prosecco, eat wedding cake, talk for hours.

*

PALIMPSEST

I had not noticed how frail you are, but at night your hands now pluck at the woolen blanket in your sleep. In the morning over breakfast, you lean slightly toward me, for confirmation of something you thought you knew, for that need for words to sound as though written in stone. After you've drunk your cup of gunpowder tea and eaten your buttered toast, you hope I won't notice the drops and crumbs spilled down your front, missing entirely the napkin I placed so carefully on your lap.

I wish I'd told you years ago about that first kiss you deliberately placed on my lips when as usual I thought you would kiss my cheek. It stayed with me for a week. Every morning of that week I woke and ran my fingers across my lips to check if you were still there. I wish I'd told you. I wish I'd told you I knew it was love when I let your dog sleep on my head.

These days we wake early. I see your mouth tremble when you turn to me, looking for words to describe the dawn thrusting its way in through the curtains, drawn against the sunlight. And the day when I couldn't find you anywhere in the house. I thought you were lost in the walls. And then I lifted the curtain and spied you through the window, outside in the rose garden, ambling among the fallen petals.

THE PICKLING OF LIMES

You are a fallen crop
Key lime yellow
I'm throwing you together
Away from the shaded grove of trees
To pickle you as if
You are Indian limes.

It will take two weeks
I quarter you, I blanket you
Wrinkled rind, corpulent flesh
Crimped seeds
With rock salt, dried chili powder
Turmeric

Cane sugar cast for balance
Burnish you under the sun.

I unscrew the stiffened lid
The old Mason jar smells faintly
Of apricots.

A friend from Chennai calls
Asks if she can visit next month
Tells me lime and lemon are
Just one word—neemboo.

Sun-soaked, slick with oil, fermented
I will add ingredients foreign to me—
Fenugreek seeds, roasted and ground
Hing powder, black mustard seeds
Sputtered in sesame oil.

Let the oil kiss your skin
As you age, you will taste
Fiery hot, a feast
Of chicken biryani, eaten with our hands
A glass of chilled Kingfisher
I pray my friend will stay awhile.

FOURTEEN WAYS OF LOOKING, BY A RHINO
(After Wallace Stevens—Thirteen Ways of Looking at a Blackbird)

I.
Do you know me?
My skin cools down when
I wallow in water-soaked mud.

II.
I roam across wild plains,
graze on grasses, pluck
leaves and fruit from branches.

III.
You have closed the corridors
that connect wide spaces—while
you farm, I search for a mate.

IV.
My horn, made from hair, grows
throughout my life. If you saw
it off with care, I will stay alive.

V.
Yet here's how it works—
if you spot me, I will soon die,
pointless trying to escape your gun.

VI.
If I stand very still
under the canopy of an acacia tree,
I might become a shadow.

VII.
When I stand unmoving
you can kill me with ease.
Am I the last of my kind?

VIII.
Oxpecker, sit on my back,
eat any insect crawling on my skin,
call out when danger comes.

IX.
I snort with anger when harassed,
run away when you come too close,
am unsafe in open grassland.

X.
I can't see too far,
the plain is vast, dusty but
I hear the shot coming.

XI.
I drop down slowly, take
my last breath on the parched earth.
Watch clouds seep over the hill.

XII.
My heart is huge—
when it stops beating
its weight rests against my ribs.

XIII.
You walk away chuckling,
my bloody horn leaking from your bag—
how many do you carry?

XIV.
Crush my horn to powder,
sell for more than gold or cocaine.
My death, a vulture's feast.

FORNICATING PIGEONS

are loud, insistent,
sound *tunk, tunk, tunk*
against the frosted glass.

The circular window has been
shuttered for months now, secured
against the contaminated outside air.

I think they want to come in,
but *tunk* turns out to be the passionate
by-product of a ritual mating dance.

Their cooing grows ever more raucous.
Their fanned wings beat in iambic pentameter.

I pause in reading to you,
look up from the book, murmur

Dearest, those pigeons are rather distracting.

LET NOT LIGHT

Over coffee one morning,
my husband looks up & says,

>   *you have stars in your eyes.*

He follows this cliché with

>   *it's too late for you to shine.*

Hesitant in his meanness,
his voice shakes a little.

He needs to stick it to me.
I want to tell him, but don't,

>   *there are no stars in my eyes—*

>   *it just looks that way to you because*
>   *I've swallowed the moon.*

DIVORCED BECAUSE OF POETRY

I creep downstairs at 2 am,
steal the keys to your boy-racer car—
the keys you *always* leave on the granite counter

because
it *never* occurred to you that I would.

*

And what a sight am I, driving
a silver-grey Jaguar in my striped pajamas,
and high-heeled vintage Manolos.

I have to laugh out loud, I have to shove
the gear-stick into 'Sports' mode.

I have to careen around jagged-uphill-bends
not meant for a night ride in a hipster mobile.

I stop where the road becomes impossibly narrow,

to the right the valley, ablaze with neon,
to the left the ocean, oily, luminous
with stars and a golden rim of moon.

An hour later, sated, I drive
down the mountain, words in my head
        jumping,
rutting,
        locking antlers—

a poem just blowing to be laid down on paper.

*

And there you are at the kitchen table—
your elbows staked out on my journal.

I toss the keys down in front of you,
they land in a place between love and hate.
I kick off my stilettos before heading up to bed.

You never even clock my smile,
and the last words I ever say to you:

    Darling, we have raccoons in the attic again.

Have you EVER?
(Questions from the Application for U. S. Citizenship)

Have you EVER been a habitual drunkard?
> Never after eleven o'clock in the morning.

Have you EVER been a prostitute or procured anyone for prostitution?
> Everyone has a price, my dear, desperation is a sour bedfellow.

Have you EVER been married to more than one person at the same time?
> Not technically, not on the same continent.

If the law requires it, are you willing to perform work of national importance under civilian direction?
> Would that include prostitution?

Have you EVER been a member of, or in any way, been associated with the Communist Party?
> Not technically, not on the same continent.

Have you EVER been a member of, or in any way, associated with a terrorist organization?
> Everyone has a price, my dear, desperation is a sour bedfellow.

Were you EVER involved in any way with killing or trying to kill someone?
> Only when I found out my commie husband was still married to someone else.

Were you EVER involved in any way with badly hurting, or trying to hurt a person, on purpose?
> As I said, only when I found out my husband was also married to someone else.

Did you EVER sell, give, or provide weapons to any person?
    It was just a small pistol given to that bastard's other wife.

Have you EVER committed, assisted in committing, or attempted to commit a crime or offense for which you were NOT arrested?
    No. No.
    I don't think so…
    No.

PERPETUALLY UNMASKED

He stomps across the lawn,
crushes grass underfoot, stops

> *Oranges and lemons,*
> *Say the bells of St. Clement's.*

by the burnt boarded-up church,
his platform a pallet of red bricks.

> *You owe me three farthings,*
> *Say the bells of St. Martin's.*

Holds aloft a Bible, upside down,
doesn't care about desecration.

> *When will you pay me?*
> *Say the bells at Old Bailey.*

He takes two tiny steps forward,
one back, readies himself to speak.

> *When I grow rich,*
> *Say the bells at Shoreditch.*

Photo-op by any means possible,
by force if necessary,

> *When will that be?*
> *Say the bells of Stepney.*

no exceptions allowed—
the path previously cleared with

> *I do not know,*
> *Says the great bell at Bow.*

tear gas, smoke flashbangs, gas canisters,
rubber bullets, batons, pepper balls.

> *Here comes a candle to light you to bed,*
> *And here comes a chopper to chop off your head!*
>
> *Chip chop chip chop.*

CASE # 1803

Unaccompanied Migrant Child,
                        forgive me—
I'm so tired these days, so many unresolved cases,
so many lost children.

Your mugshot showed you staring
straight ahead, unsmiling.

Unidentified Migrant Child,
                        it took me months
to locate you in San Antonio.

The warehouse lights shining 24/7
made it easy to find you
beneath the concrete bench, just your eyes
lifting from a crumpled tin-foil blanket,

In one hand you held a picture
of the Statue of Liberty,
half-colored with three broken crayons
a new friend passed through the wire mesh.

You told me later this place has two names,
you children call it "The Dog Kennel,"
the guards call it "The Freezer"—always cold,
yet they took your sweater away from you.

A man in a uniform
let you use the blue crayon
you'd folded tight in your fist
to sign your name on the release.

A woman in a uniform
carried you curled up
onto an empty school bus,
drove you to the Hampton Inn,

had you shower, zapped your hair
with an electric lice comb,
braided it with a frayed red ribbon.

Gabriela, Beloved Migrant Child,
you were asleep by the time we left,
didn't utter a sound as we crossed the border,
slept all the way to Leon, looked dazed
when I shook you awake.

I told you Mami and Papa couldn't wait
to see you, Abuela too.

But now when I phone,
Mami says you scare her at night
when you creep into Abuela's bedroom
to sleep in her closet,

and Papa is angry
when you circle him, when you mutter
over and over,

>   *Don't make it hard on yourself, kid.*

Because for a whole year after, it's all you can say.

DRIVING ON PICO BLVD.

I should keep my eyes on the road driving on Pico because in LA we do much more in our cars than just drive. At one time or another, more than half of us have driven with our knees. I'm still working on steering with one hand, elbow casually crooked at the open window.

Driving next to me a woman smiles to herself while multi-tasking—full-volume raven-black mascara, low volume Gregorian chant, an iced decaf oat milk latte (no soy milk, she carries the BRCA gene) (no almond milk, she's heard there's a drought in the State).

The man behind me puts down his nose-hair trimmer as I watch him in the rear-view mirror, picks up his phone to text the woman he is going to meet (not his wife, she is at that moment placing her hand over the real estate agent's hand in another house fresh on the over-heated LA market).

I should be aware of the traffic ahead, and behind, but I'm distracted by the growing pile of trash discarded on the sidewalk. I'm not talking everyday litter—faded receipts, cigarette butts, hard lumps of gum, plastic popsicle sticks, a crap-filled diaper.

Instead, I observe the fifties porcelain toilet bowl, a seatless, three-legged wicker-back chair, one mud-caked and blood-smeared sneaker, a stained sofa-bed with a cushion carefully placed at one end, the corpse of a Christmas tree flocked with artificial snow and wrapped head-to-toe in plastic.

Stopped at the lights, alternating between podcasts, 'Death, Sex & Money' and 'On Being,' I idly wonder what time of day will it be when I spot a lifeless body right there in the trash at the side of the road? Whether I'll have time to pull over, park, and take a photo before I call 911.

WE WILL NOT BE QUIET
*After Rev. James Lawson Jr.'s speech
at the funeral of Congressman John Lewis.*

We will no longer be quiet though
we crouch before fists raised high.

While our books are being burned,
come sing our childhood hymns.

In the lambent light of bonfires
set all across the country,

our children twirl, feverish,
engulfed by the famished smoke.

We will not be quiet even as
the baskets of our hearts are emptied
of all that we recognize.

Let us speak the exact noisy truth
until our *good trouble* is finished,
neither let silence become endangered.

Before I'm taken from you, my love,
give me the gift of your words.

Then cut me into stars and hide me
far in the seething night sky.

CONFINEMENT

Over sixty (high risk they say),
my days alone are managed over the phone,
in conversations with family and friends.

This morning from her apartment
in Chinatown, LA my daughter calls,
her tears cup in my hands.

Mom, how long does the virus live on your skin?

*A man spat on me today,
called me chink,
told me to fuck off back to China.*

*Mom, do you know why the media
don't show us how
we're going to die from it?*

*Don't tell us our lungs disintegrate,
don't show
a mother in her hospital bed,*

*head flopped sideways,
a rush of blood into her lungs,
as her heart stops.*

Mom, dry your tears and listen to me.

EMERGENCY ROOM
After Wislawa Szymborska, Funeral (II)

"He's going to give you a tuna sandwich to see if you vomit."
"I need a second doctor to sign off on my right to die."
"It's not a chocolate pudding, it's a chocolate tart, it cost me $38."
"The hairy guy in the next cubicle is really hot."
"Are you experiencing fever over 100, difficulty breathing, or a cough?"
"I keep seeing him staring at me as he went under the car."
"I can't sign the fucking form with handcuffs on, you moron."
"You sound as lucid as I do after 36 hours on call."
"I got pee on the outside of the cup, and it's smudged my name."
"You're 72 and you haven't signed up for Medicare?"
"Are you done yet? The restaurant closes at 10 pm."
"ON A SCALE OF 1—10 HOW IS YOUR HEARING?"
"Next time, call 1-800-LUNGUSA before you come."
"You've got a phone call about your dog."
"Do you have thoughts of harming yourself?"
"I'm her mother."
"I'm his husband."
"I'm her housekeeper."
"The meter will run out soon."
"I think he's dead."
"You can leave after we reboot the system."

THE RECKONING

What will you and I talk about
when there's nothing left to say?

When our dog stops barking
from behind the ficus hedge.

When groceries aren't delivered,
when we have no tips left to give.

When we understand
that hunger is not our enemy.

When we forget how to bandage
the broken wing of a sparrow.

When all houses of worship
are limited to true believers.

When we are at the end of our ropes
even as fear keeps us tethered.

When we are frozen in the act
of looking backward—

What will you and I talk about then?

NEW CALIFORNIA

To the gun-store they march, all legs and death
pressed to the pavement. Mask-less, they join a line

that stretches 'round the block, buying bullets
and guns, before the dealer runs out of stock.

This is the new California
where Shelter-In-Place means:

take your gun apart in your garage,
clean it, oil it, let the bullets rip up the dry dirt.

I would trade toilet paper for white wine, but
not for a shot at my neighbor, though the Trump sign
in his yard shouts "Promises Made, Promises Kept."

I think, maybe I should go for a hike,
or perhaps head off to a firing range
to learn how to shoot for myself.

I make a decision, shop online, have a coffin
flown overnight from BestBuyCaskets.com,
park it in the garage alongside my car:

a White Angel coffin, lacquered with rose-gold
accessories, an Eternal Rest adjustable mattress,
with matching pink pillow and throw.

One thing I know. My casket is breathtaking.

It is not a good time to go hiking. Gun-shy,
I stay at home, follow the rules, wash my hands,
eat caramel popcorn, wash my hands, watch old movies—

my favorite is *Dirty Harry*, though *John Wick* comes
a close second, despite the death of Daisy his dog.

THANK YOU

I would like to thank Douglas Manuel and Carolyne Wright for taking time out of their busy schedules to read my manuscript, and so cordially agree to write the blurbs for this book. Some of the poems in this chapbook originated in their workshops, and they continue to inspire me.

I stand in awe of Justen Ahren—poet, photographer, musician and so much more. I am deeply appreciative of his willingness to share his art and allow the use of one of his photographs from his recent series, *The Earth Tends To Beauty Despite*, for the cover of this book.

To my dear friend, and fellow poet, Chris (C.W. Emerson) the gift of your presence in my life is immeasurable. You are my music.

www.ingramcontent.com/pod-product-compliance
Lightning Source LLC
LaVergne TN
LVHW041602070426
835507LV00011B/1267